FRANK P. HAGGARD

APRIL 19 1993

AF411885

THE EARTH BEING ROUND

To Eric and Nanette Asimov

LONGMAN GROUP LIMITED
Longman House
Burnt Mill, Harlow, Essex, UK

Text © Isaac Asimov 1972
Illustrations © Longman Group Limited 1983

First published in the United States of America
in 1972 by the Walker Publishing Company, Inc.
This edition first published 1983
Illustrated by Bob Chapman
Cover design by David Brown
ISBN 0 582 39162 8

Set in 12/14pt Baskerville VIP

*Printed and bound in Great Britain by
William Clowes (Beccles) Limited, Beccles and London*

Contents

Flat Earth under a bowl as a sky

1. Is the Earth flat?

Far back in ancient times, everybody thought the Earth was flat. This is because it looks flat.

If you are in a boat way out in the middle of the ocean, the top of the water looks flat in every direction and the sky seems to fit over it like an upside-down bowl. The line where the sky and water meet is called the "horizon". The horizon looks like a circle with you yourself at the centre.

If you are on land, the land stretches out to a horizon also. The horizon on land, however, is not even. It goes up and down because of houses, trees, hills, and other things.

Some ancient people suspected the Earth went on forever. They thought it might be a huge flat piece of land and sea with no end at all.

But if this was the case, then what about the Sun? The Sun rose in the east in the morning. It travelled across the sky and set in the west in the evening. Then the next morning, it rose again in the east.

Some ancient people tried to explain this by saying that every morning, a brand new Sun was manufactured and rose. When it set, it was destroyed.

Others said that the Sun set in the ocean to the west. Then during the night, it was put in a boat and rowed to the east. By morning, it was ready to rise again.

Still others thought the Sun was a golden, flaming chariot pulled by magic horses that could fly through the air. In the morning, the sun-god would get into the chariot in the east. Then he and his horses would climb through the air, reaching the top of the sky at noon. They would then race downwards, reaching the far western ground in the evening. Somehow the sun-god would get back to the east during the night when his golden, flaming chariot gave out no light.

Stars that were very far from the North Star moved in such big circles that those circles dipped below the horizon. Those stars rose in the east and set in the west.

The Moon also travelled across the sky from east to west. So did the stars. These things also had to be explained. The ancient explanations just didn't make sense.

Suppose we have a flat Earth stretching out in every direction. How deep is it? Suppose you begin to dig a hole. Can you keep on digging forever, going down and down without end?

Or is the Earth just a slab of material, maybe a kilometre thick—or 10 kilometres—or 50 kilometres? If it is just a slab of material, what keeps it from falling down?

The people who lived in India in ancient times decided the Earth didn't fall because it was resting on huge elephants. But what were the elephants standing on? They said all the elephants were standing on the back of gigantic turtles.

What was the turtle standing on?

They said it was swimming in a tremendous ocean.

Indian belief

Well, then, did the ocean stretch all the way down? There was no answer to that.

So you see, while the Earth *looks* flat, it may not be safe to decide that it is flat.

The first people who thought about the problems of the flat Earth were certain Greeks who lived about 2,500 years ago on what is now the western coast of the nation of Turkey.

One of them was a man named Anaximander. He wasn't satisfied with the tales of sun-gods and flaming chariots and flying horses. Instead, he looked at the night sky and asked himself what he really saw.

On a clear night, he saw the stars. During the night they seemed to travel across the sky.

One star, however, didn't move. It was the North Star. It stayed in the same place in the northern sky all night long. It stayed there night after night. The stars near it moved in a circle around it. If the stars were very near it, they moved in small circles. If they were further away, they moved in bigger circles.

The most important thing about the night sky to Anaximander was that the stars travelled in patterns. They weren't like a swarm of bees, in which each bee moves its own way. Instead, all the stars moved together.

Anaximander decided that the sky was a huge hollow ball, or "sphere". The sphere of the sky turned around on an invisible line or "axis". One end of the axis was where the North Star was situated. The other end was at the opposite end of the sphere where he couldn't see it.

Everyday, the sphere of the sky turned around, or "rotated". The stars were all stuck to the sky and turned with it. That's why they kept the same pattern. The Sun and Moon were stuck to the sky, too, and that's why they

Sphere of the sky around a central axis

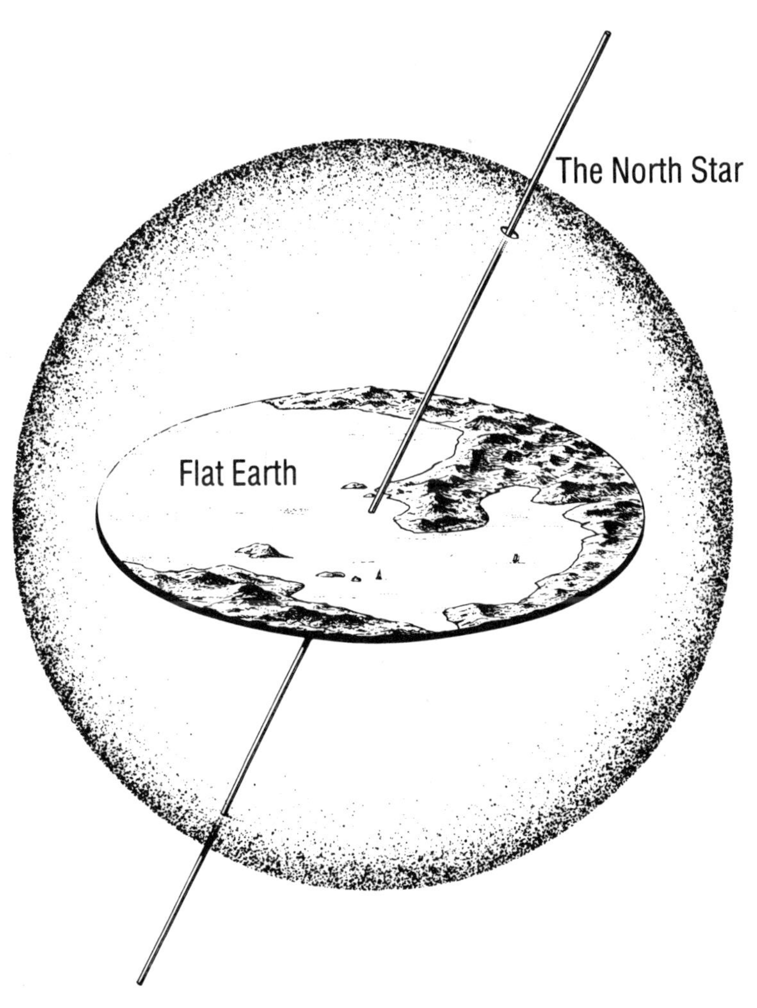

rose and set.

Even though the sky was a sphere, it was still possible for the Earth to be flat. Anaximander thought it was a flat slab that stretched across the sphere of the sky at its centre.

As the sphere of the sky turned, the Sun rose in the east, travelled across the sky, and set in the west. The turning sky carried it along. Then as the sky kept turning, the Sun was carried to the bottom part of the sphere. When the Sun shone on the bottom side of the slab of the Earth, it was night. When the turning sky carried the Sun around to the east, it rose and it was day again. The Moon and the stars also moved in this way. Anaximander's idea made more sense than the ideas of earlier thinkers. The Sun was not destroyed each night nor was it rowed from west to east. Yet Anaximander wasn't satisfied. He kept on thinking.

2. The disappearing stars

If the Earth was a flat slab that fitted tightly across the middle of the sphere of the sky, we could travel to the place where the Earth and sky met. We could reach the place where the Sun rose in the east and we could reach out and touch it (unless its heat killed us).

If we travelled far enough to the west, we could reach the place where the Sun set.

Some people, centuries ago, really thought this could be done. They even drew pictures showing a man coming to the place where the sky touched the Earth. They showed the man with his head through the sky, looking at the machinery that kept the sphere of the sky turning.

The ancient Greek thinkers, however, didn't really believe that. After all, no matter how far to the east or west people travelled, they never seemed to get any closer to the Sun, the Moon, or the stars.

Perhaps, then, the Earth didn't stretch from one side of the sky to the other. Perhaps our eyes only fooled us when they showed the sky touching the Earth at the horizon.

Maybe the Earth was a flat disc that was quite large but was far smaller than the sphere of the sky. If this was the case, the Sun, the Moon, and the stars would be far away from the edge of the Earth. No one on Earth would be able to reach them or even get particularly close to them.

But if the Earth was a flat disc in the centre of the sphere of the sky, with the sky far away on all sides, then why didn't travellers reach the end of the Earth?

Perhaps because the land portion of the Earth was in the middle of the flat disc and was surrounded by water. Travellers always reached the ocean, if they travelled far enough. It was the ocean, then, that stretched out to the end of the Earth. People, in ancient times, didn't travel far out of sight of land. Maybe that was why they never came to the end of the Earth.

But then why didn't the water of the ocean spill off the end of the Earth?

Maybe the end of the Earth was turned up at the edge, so that the water was held in. Maybe the Earth wasn't exactly a flat slab, but was a shallow bowl.

In that case, why didn't the whole Earth simply fall?

It was still hard to consider the Earth as flat, even if the sky was a huge sphere and the problem of sunrise and sunset was explained.

If the Earth isn't flat, what other shape can it be?

Suppose we look at the sky again. In the sky, there are many shining objects, most of which are stars. Stars are just little points of light to the eye and the ancient thinkers couldn't tell anything about them.

Two objects in the sky are different, however. They are the Sun and the Moon.

The Sun is a circle of light at all times, but the Moon isn't. Sometimes, it *is* a circle of light, but sometimes it is only half a circle. Sometimes it is in between a whole circle

Earth as a shallow bowl

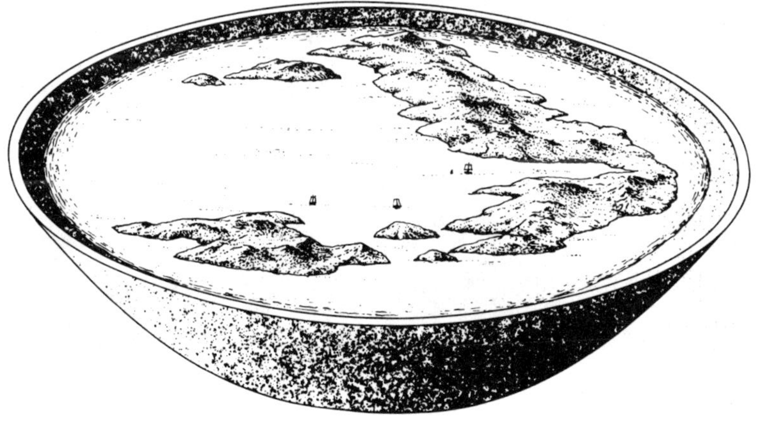

Phases of the Moon

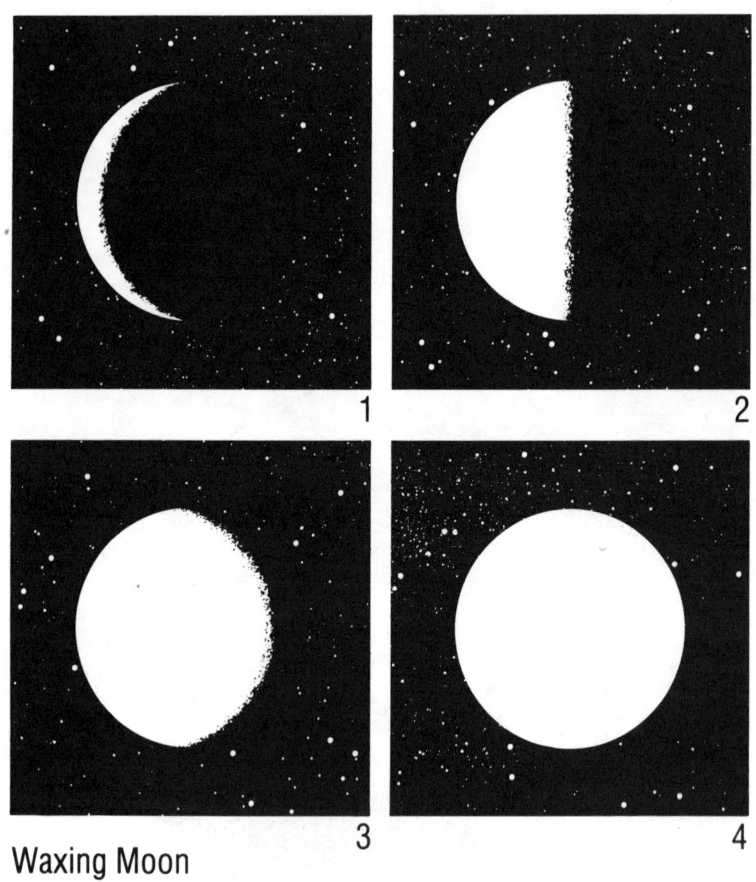

Waxing Moon

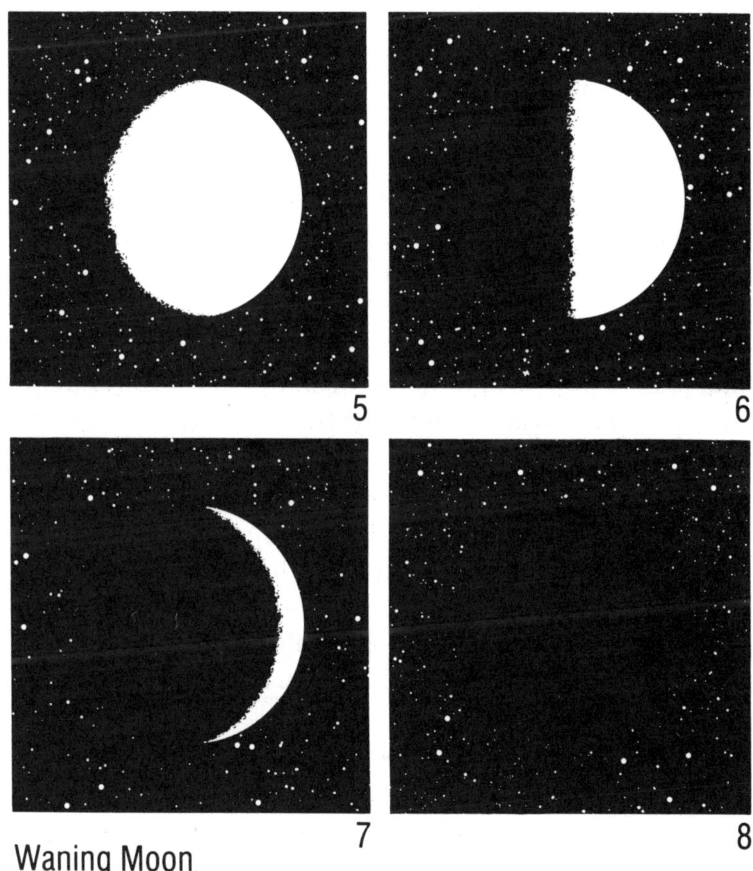

5
6
7
8
Waning Moon

and half a circle. Sometimes it is just a thin curve of light called a "crescent".

The Greeks who watched the Moon, night after night, noticed that it changed its position in respect to the Sun. They noticed that as it changed its position, it also changed its shape.

When the Moon and Sun were on opposite sides of the Earth, the Moon was always a full circle of light. The Sun shone past the Earth onto the Moon. It lit up the whole side of the Moon.

When the Moon and the Sun were on the same side of the Earth, they couldn't see the Moon at all. The Sun shone on the other side of the Moon, the side they couldn't see. The side they could see received no sunlight and it was dark.

The ancient scholars who observed this decided the Sun had light of its own and the Moon didn't. The Moon shone only because it was lit up by the Sun. The Moon shone by "reflected light".

The ancient Greeks had begun to work out the study of "geometry", which deals with the shapes of objects. They considered the different shapes of the lighted part of the Moon. They considered the half-moons, the crescent-moons, and other types. They could easily show that in order for the lighted part of the Moon to take on the shapes it did, the Moon had to be a round ball, or sphere.

The what about the shape of the Sun? It shone on the Moon and it did so equally well from all angles. Whether the Moon and Sun were on opposite sides of the Earth, or on the same side, or anything in between, the Moon received the same kind of light on the side that faced the Sun. This could only have happened if the Sun was a sphere.

With all this in mind, Anaximander could see that there

were three objects in the sky that had a particular shape. There was the Sun, the Moon, and the whole sky itself. All three were spheres.

Did that mean that the Earth was also a sphere? Did that mean the Earth was round instead of flat?

Not necessarily. Maybe the rules were different for the sky and Earth. Just because the sky and a few objects in the sky were spheres didn't mean that the Earth had to be a sphere. After all, the Sun was hot and blazing but the Earth wasn't. The Moon moved through the sky, but the Earth didn't seem to. The sky itself was full of stars, but the Earth wasn't.

No, in order to decide upon the shape of the Earth, people had to consider the Earth itself, and not other objects.

So let's go back to the Earth and ask ourselves the following question: would we see the stars differently from different parts of the Earth?

We wouldn't if the Earth was flat. Suppose we looked at the sky at night. We would see all the stars in the sky above us if the night was clear. If we were anywhere else on a flat Earth, we would still see those same stars.

But that is not the way things really are!

There were many people, in ancient times, who had to travel. People who travelled north would notice that the sky at night seemed a little different. Some stars that they used to see near the southern horizon when they were at home couldn't be seen at all when they went northwards. Then, when they returned home, those stars they hadn't been able to see showed up again just above the southern horizon.

People who travelled southwards found things just the opposite. When they went south, they could make out stars just above the southern horizon that they never saw

Earth as a cylinder

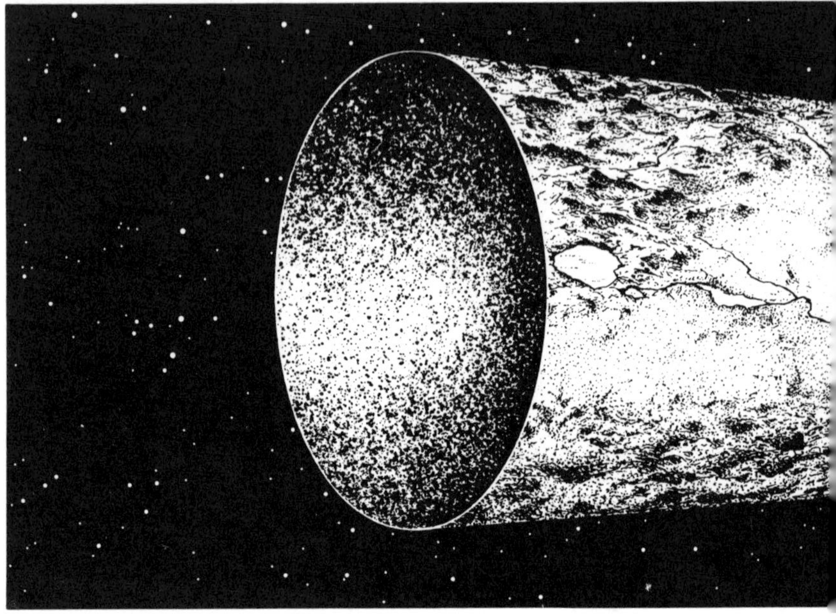

at home. When they returned, those stars disappeared again.

This was true of the northern horizon, too. At home, some stars dipped just a little below the northern horizon as they turned with the sky. If one travelled north, those stars stayed just a little above it. If one travelled south, stars which stayed just a little above the northern horizon when one was at home began to dip below it.

The fact of the matter was that the stars were not seen from all parts of the Earth, so the Earth could not be flat.

Maybe the Earth was shaped like a tin can, or "cylinder". This is exactly how Anaximander thought the Earth might be shaped. He thought it was a cylinder lying in the centre of the sphere of the sky. When you went

14

north, you travelled along the curve of the cylinder. When you looked back, the curve hid some of the stars to the south. If you went south, you also travelled along the curve of the cylinder. When you looked back, the curve hid some of the stars to the north.

That explained the difference in the appearance of the sky as you went from place to place.

3. The disappearing ships

Anaximander's theory of a cylindrical Earth raises some questions.

First, if the Earth is cylindrical, why does it look flat?

That's not hard to answer. The Earth is so large and we're so small that we can only see a tiny part of it as we look around. The curve is so slight on a very tiny part of the Earth that the surface looks flat.

To see this, imagine a large balloon blown up until it is 1 metre across. Imagine a tiny circle on the balloon 1 centimetre across. If a tiny insect could see only that much of the balloon, the surface of the balloon would appear flat.

Here is a second question that's harder to answer. If you are travelling down a curve when you go northwards or southwards why don't you feel as though you are walking downhill? Why don't you start to slide?

You might think that the ground is so rough that it prevents you from sliding. But what if you're not travelling over rough ground? What if you travel by ship

A tiny circle on a sphere looks flat

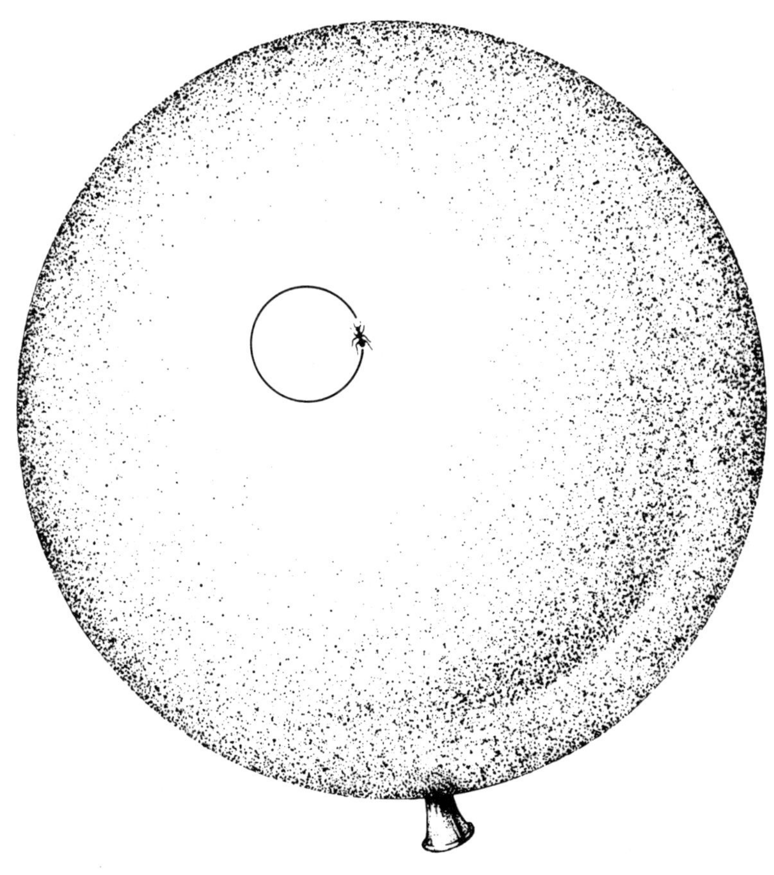

Ships disappearing over the horizon

northwards or southwards over the smooth ocean? Why doesn't the ship start sliding forward? In fact, why doesn't the whole ocean just slide downwards and all its water pour right off the Earth.

Anaximander didn't have a good answer for that. He just felt that there was no other way to explain the appearance of the night sky than to suppose the Earth had a cylindrical shape.

Why does the Earth curve only if we go north and south? Suppose we go east and west. Does the appearance of the stars change? Do stars disappear behind the western horizon if we go east? Do they disappear behind the eastern horizon if we go west?

That's hard to tell. Since the sky turns, stars are always

18

appearing at the eastern horizon and disappearing at the western horizon. Travelling east and west doesn't change that.

If the sky stopped rotating, it would be possible to tell whether stars were appearing and disappearing in the east and west. But the sky never stops rotating for even a moment, so that's no help.

But it's not very good to make a decision just because you have no evidence. To prove something, you need evidence.

Perhaps there's some other way of getting information about the shape of the Earth, some way that doesn't involve the sky and the way it turns.

That kind of information can be obtained on the

seashore and does not involve the sky.

If the Earth was flat, a ship would get smaller and smaller as it sailed further and further away from shore. Finally, it would become a dot and disappear.

This, however, is not what happens. To begin with, someone watching a ship sail away can see the whole ship. He or she sees the wooden hull of the ship below and the sails above. After a while, however, the hull disappears. The water seems to reach above it and all that is left are the sails. Then only the top of the sails. Then the whole ship disappears.

Can it be that the ship is sinking? Is the water rising higher and higher, covering first the hull and then the sails?

That can't be, since it happens to every ship that sails away and most of them return safely. When a ship returned in ancient times, the sailors swore that at no time did the water rise above the hull.

How else could this be explained?

There was one way. Suppose the Earth's surface curved. The ship would then sail away over that curve and would gradually disappear behind it. Naturally, the bottom part would disappear first.

The ships were hidden by the curve of the Earth, just as the stars near the horizon were hidden.

But there was one great difference. You could see the stars disappear behind the curve of the Earth only if you travelled north and south. In other directions, the turning of the sky spoiled things.

The ships, on the other hand, disappeared bottom first in *whatever* direction they went. They disappeared bottom first, whether they went north, south, east, west, or any direction in between.

What's more, it always looked as though they

A sphere curves equally in all directions

disappeared at about the same rate. If they were three kilometres away, a certain amount of hull was hidden, no matter in what direction they were sailing.

It looked as though the Earth curved in *every* direction, and by the same amount in every direction.

But the *only* shape that curves by the same amount in every direction is a sphere. If you make a point on a large ball and draw lines away from that point in any direction, you will see that all the lines will curve in the same way.

Judging by what happens to ships, the Earth is not a cylinder, but a sphere. It is a large sphere in the centre of the much larger sphere of the sky. If the Earth is a large sphere, then the tiny bit we can see at any one time looks flat.

But that still leaves us with the question of why we don't slip off the Earth when we move around and why the air and ocean don't slip off. Is there something else that can give us proof of the Earth's shape? There is something, but for that we have to go back to the sky again.

4. The Earth's shadow

Every once in a while, the Moon loses its light. A black shadow moves across it until all one can see is a dim red glow. After a while, the shadow moves away and the Moon is back again, shining as brightly as ever.

When this happens, the Moon is said to be "eclipsed".

In ancient times, an eclipse of the Moon frightened people. They thought the Moon might remain dark forever and they did not want to lose the Moon's helpful light at night.

Those who studied the sky carefully were sure this would not happen. They noticed, for instance, that an eclipse took place only at the time of the full Moon. It never took place at any other time. What's more it only took place during certain full moons.

The ancient Greeks who studied the sky knew that when the Moon was full, it was on the opposite side of the Earth from the Sun. The Sun shone past the Earth onto the Moon. The Sun lit up the entire side facing them and that is why the Greeks saw the Moon as a full, round circle

Cavedweller watching eclipse of the Moon

of light.

Suppose, however, that the Earth was *exactly* in between the Moon and Sun. Then the sunlight would have to go through the Earth to reach the Moon. It couldn't do that, of course, so no light would reach the Moon.

Another way of saying this is that the Earth casts a shadow. During an eclipse, the Earth's shadow falls on the Moon and darkens it. Every once in a while, at the time of the full moon, the Earth is exactly in between the Moon and the Sun, and at those times there is an eclipse.

When the Earth casts a shadow on the Moon, we can find out something about the shape of the Earth. The first thing we notice is that the edge of its shadow is a curve that looks exactly like part of a circle.

The Greeks watched eclipses of the Moon that took place in different parts of the sky. They watched eclipses when the Moon was high in the sky, or low, or at the horizon. When the Moon was in different positions during an eclipse, the sunlight struck the Earth from different angles. The shape of the shadow never changed. No matter where the Moon was during the eclipse, the Earth's shadow, as it moved across the Moon, always looked like part of a circle.

This meant that the Earth had a shape that cast a circular shadow in every possible direction. There is only one shape that does that, and that shape is a sphere.

About 450 BC, a Greek scholar named Philolaus, who lived in southern Italy, was finally convinced. He put all the evidence together. The change in the stars, the way in which ships disappeared as they moved away, and the shadow of the Earth during an eclipse of the Moon led him to one conclusion: the Earth was a sphere located in the centre of the much larger sphere of the sky.

So far as we know, Philolaus was the first person ever to

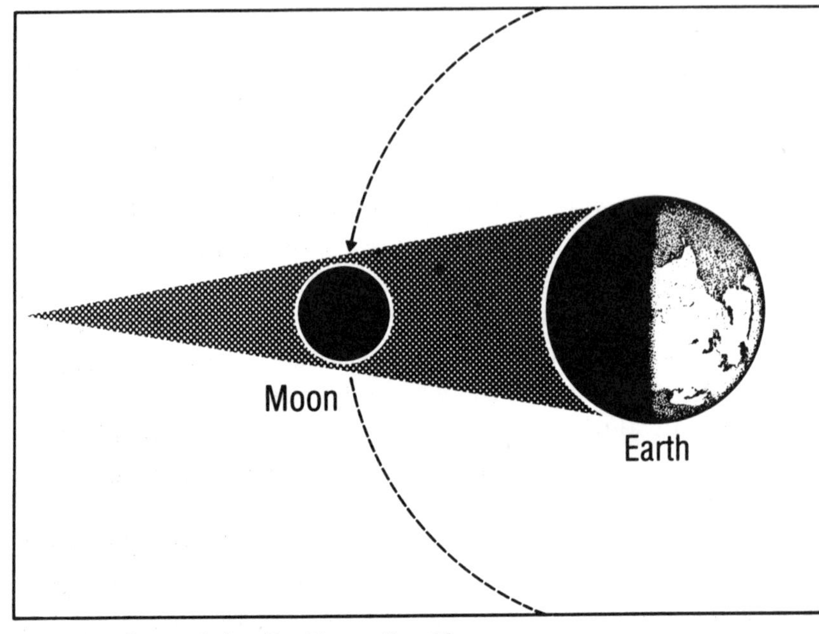

The shadow of the Earth on the Moon

say that the Earth was a sphere.

But that still left unanswered questions. If the Earth was a sphere and we were all living on top of it, why didn't we slide off as soon as we moved away from the top. Why didn't the ocean drip off and all the air drift away?

Let's thing about this a little. Things fall downwards. If we drop something, down it goes. But what do we mean by "down"? If the Earth is a sphere and something falls down, it is falling towards the centre of the Earth.

This is true for every person on Earth, no matter where he or she is standing. A person may be on one side of the sphere of the Earth, or on the opposite side, or anywhere in between. Wherever they are, that person and

26

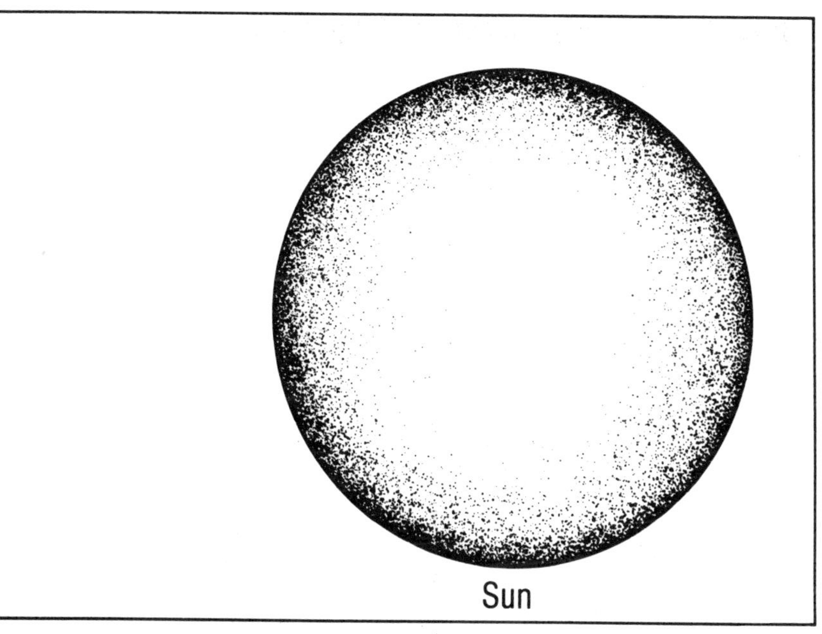

everything else about them are attracted to the centre of the Earth. Wherever they are standing, the centre is always in the direction of their feet, so that their feet seem to be "down" and their heads "up".

About 350 BC, the Greek scholar, Aristotle, pointed this out clearly.

Aristotle's view that everything was attracted towards the centre of the Earth meant that the Earth *had* to be a sphere.

This explains why the oceans and air stay on the spherical Earth, and don't slide or drop off. Wherever they are, they are pulled "down" towards the centre.

"Down" is towards the centre of the Earth

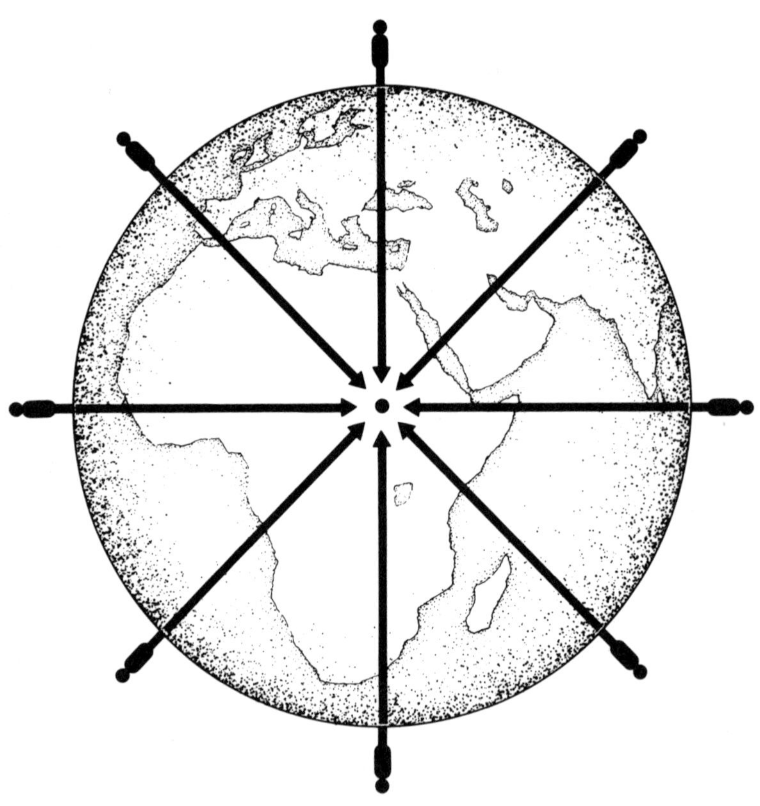

5.   The size of the Earth

After Aristotle's time, scholars agreed that the Earth was a sphere. How big was that sphere?

One way a person could tell was by walking. If you walked till you have travelled all round the sphere and come back to the place where you started and if you kept track of how far you went, you would know the size of the Earth.

But there was no way of doing this. If a person walked in any direction, they would eventually come to the ocean. To keep on going they would have to sail for thousands of kilometres across the ocean. The Greeks didn't have the kind of ships that could sail that far.

Was there any way of finding out the size of the Earth while staying at home? A Greek scholar named Eratosthenes found such a way about 240 BC.

This is how he thought it out . . .

If the Earth is a sphere, sunlight must hit different parts of it at different angles. Suppose that in the part of the world where you are, the Sun is directly overhead at a particular time, so that sunlight shines straight down on you. But the sphere of the Earth curves, so that sunlight hitting the ground at a place hundreds of kilometres from you has to come down at a slant. The further a place is from you, the greater the slant at which sunlight must hit. You can measure the slant by the shadow it casts.

Suppose you have a wooden rod stuck upright into the ground. If the sunlight is coming from directly above, straight down, the rod casts no shadow. If the sunlight is coming at a slight slant, the rod casts a short shadow. The greater the slant, the longer the shadow.

In that case, imagine wooden rods of the same size stuck into the ground in two places 800 kilometres apart. Suppose the Sun is directly over one of those rods at a certain time. It will cast no shadow, but the other one will cast a short shadow because sunlight reaches it at a slant.

If the sphere of the Earth is very large, the surface will curve only slightly in 800 kilometres. The sunlight will strike the other rod at only a slight slant and will cast only a very short shadow. If the sphere of the Earth is quite small, the surface will curve a larger amount in 800 kilometres and the other rod will cast a longer shadow.

From the difference in shadows at two different places on the Earth, which are a known distance apart, the size of the sphere can be calculated by geometry.

Eratosthenes was told that, at noon on 21 June, the longest day in the year, a wooden rod stuck into the Earth at Syene (a city in southern Egypt) cast no shadow. Eratosthenes worked in Alexandria, a city in northern Egypt. He knew that on that day a wooden rod stuck into the ground would cast a shadow of a certain length. He also knew that it was 800 kilometres from Syene to Alexandria.

Working with that information, he calculated that the

Size of the Earth

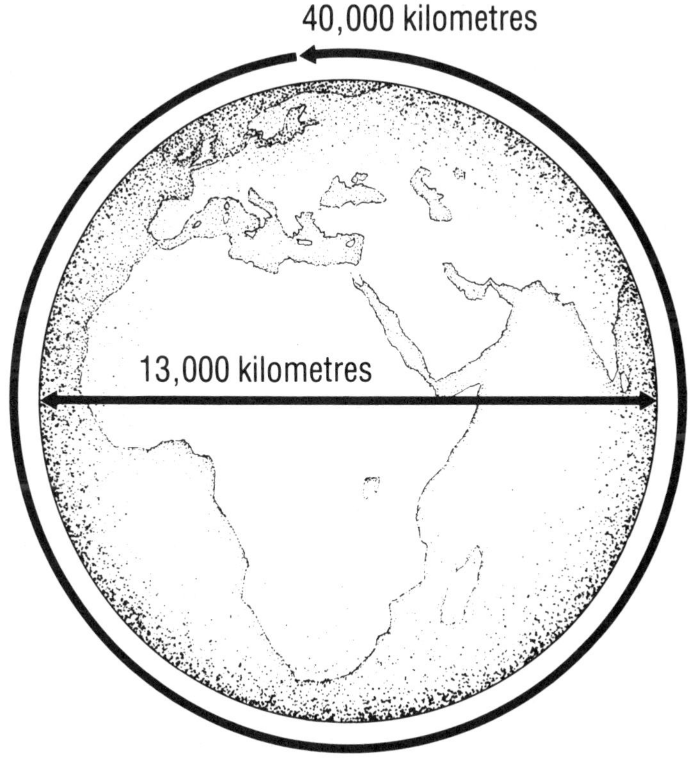

sphere of the Earth was 40,000 kilometres around (circumference), and 13,000 kilometres through the middle (diameter).

Not everybody agreed with Eratosthenes's calculations. Many Greek scholars felt he made the Earth far too large. Some made new calculations and decided the sphere of the Earth was only 29,000 kilometres round. That seemed a more comfortable figure to most of the ancient Greeks.

About 150 AD, a Greek astonomer named Ptolemy used the smaller figure in a book he wrote about geography. This book was considered the last word on the subject and for more than a thousand years scholars agreed that Ptolemy must be right.

In the 1400s, the whole question of the shape of the Earth became very important. The nations of western Europe wanted very much to trade with lands of the Far East. They wanted to trade with India, China, Japan and the islands off southeast Asia. These were all called "the Indies".

Those far-off lands had silks and spices and many things Europeans wanted. Unfortunately, there was no easy way of reaching the Indies. One could travel many thousands of kilometres over land, but travel by land was very hard in those days. Besides, most of the trip had to be made through nations hostile to Europeans.

It might be easier to reach the Indies by sea, but no one was sure how to do that. One possible way was to sail around Africa, but in those days nobody knew the size and shape of Africa. Beginning about 1418, ships set out from Portugal to explore the coast of Africa. It wasn't until 69 years later, in 1487, that a Portuguese navigator finally reached the southern end of Africa.

Meanwhile, an Italian navigator named Christopher Columbus wondered if it was necessary to go around Africa at all. It was such a long distance all the way south to the tip of Africa, then all the way north to the Indies. Maybe there was a shorter route.

It was many thousands of kilometres from the western end of Europe to the eastern end of Asia. Those thousands of kilometres of land curved around the sphere of the Earth. Maybe they curved nearly all the way around the sphere, so that they almost touched.

In that case, wouldn't it be quicker to sail directly west from Europe and reach the Indies that way?

That depended on how big the Earth was. Suppose the Earth was 40,000 kilometres in circumference, as Eratosthenes had said, and that it was 14,500 kilometres from western Europe to the Indies by land. In that case, Columbus would have to sail 25,500 kilometres west to reach Asia. There were no ships at that time that could do this.

But suppose the Earth was only 29,000 kilometres in circumference, as Ptolemy said, and 19,000 kilometres from western Europe to the Indies by land. Then it would be only a 10,000-kilometre sail across the ocean. There were supposed to be islands east of Asia and islands west of Europe. If they were taken into account, it might be only 5,000 kilometres from Europe to the Indies by boat.

Columbus persuaded the King and Queen of Spain that the distance was only 5,000 kilometres. In August 1492, he sailed westwards with three ships.

As it happened, Columbus was wrong. The Indies were much further away than he thought. What he didn't know, however, was that there were huge continents lying between Europe and Asia. The eastern edge of these continents was just about where Columbus thought the islands east of Asia were.

On 12 October 1492, Columbus reached a small island which he thought was quite near the Indies. He sailed on and explored certain larger islands which are, to this very day, called the "West Indies" because of Columbus's mistake.

Columbus called the people he found on these islands "Indians", and that's what we call the descendants of the original inhabitants of these continents today.

Although Columbus was convinced he had reached the Indies, others weren't so sure. The lands he had found were nothing at all like the descriptions that had been given by those who had travelled overland to China.

Some people thought that the lands Columbus had discovered were new continents. One of the first explorers who said this was an Italian navigator named Americus Vespucius. A German geographer, Martin Waldseemül-ler, decided Vespucius was right. In 1507, Waldseemül-ler, suggested that the new continents be called America in honour of Americus Vespucius.

By that time, Portugal had reached the Indies by sailing around Africa. Spain had reached only the new continents and these were not as wealthy or as civilised as the Indies.

There was a Portuguese navigator, however, named Ferdinand Magellan who felt he had been cheated by his government after years of loyal service. He went to Spain and told the Spanish king that there was still a way he could rech the Indies without going around Africa and having to fight the Portuguese. All that had to be done was to sail westwards *past* the Americas and keep on going.

In 1519, Magellan set sail with fleet of five ships. He came to South America and began to look for a way past it. He finally reached the southern end and travelled through a narrow passage that is called the "Straits of Magellan" to this day.

At the other end, he reached another ocean. He sailed across this ocean for weeks in calm weather. Magellan called this new body of water the Pacific Ocean because he felt this new ocean was "pacific" or peaceful. This is still its name, though the Pacific Ocean has as many storms as any other ocean.

Magellan found the Pacific Ocean was large and empty. He had to sail for 99 days without seeing land. The crew ran out of food and water and nearly died before they reached the small island of Guam and found relief.

The ships then went on to the Philippine Islands, where Magellan was killed in a quarrel with the inhabitants.

The rest of the expedition continued, however. Finally, in 1522, after a 3-year voyage, they reached Spain again. Only one ship of the original five made it and it had only 18 men left aboard.

Magellan's expedition was the first to go all around the world. His records represented the final proof of just how large the sphere of the globe was. It turned out that Eratosthenes had been correct when the made his calculations from shadows 1,800 years before.

The Earth is 40,000 kilometres in circumference. Everyone else who thought the Earth was much smaller was wrong.

Still if it hadn't been for the mistaken idea that the Earth was smaller than it was, Columbus might not have thought it was practical to sail west. America might not have been discovered by Europeans for a long time. Even mistakes can be useful.

Magellan's trip does not end the story of the Earth's shape.

Beginning in 1961, people were sent into orbit around the Earth. They began to travel longer and longer distances through space and to go further and further from Earth. By 1969, men had reached the Moon.

From outer space they could look back on Earth and see it as an object in the sky.

They could see that it was round. Pictures taken from outer space showed everyone else on Earth that their planet was round.

The Earth is round and the old Greek scholars who reasoned it out nearly 2,500 years ago by studying stars and ships and eclipses were absolutely right.

Index